MW01602079

All the Best

A devotion to choose what's best in the midst of life's pressures, demands and distractions.

collide.

© 2023 Collide

All rights reserved. No part of this book may be reproduced or transmitted in any form or by any means whatsoever without express written permission from the author, except in the case of brief quotations embodied in critical articles and reviews. Please refer all pertinent questions to the publisher.

All biblical references are from the NIV translation unless otherwise noted.

info@wecollide.net

Cover and book design by Amanda Garvin

First printing edition 2023

wecollide.net

Table of Contents

There are so many experiences calling our name, so many opportunities we could say yes to, so many dreams to chase, so many relationships to invest in. It's so easy as women to feel distracted, pulled in one hundred directions and even frantic at times.

Does worry keep you up at night? Does stress keep bossing you around? Are you trying to hold everything together and feel like you're failing?

We all resonate with the big dreams and great opportunities inviting our time, but the perfectionist in each of us is tempted to take over. We try to be amazing in so many endeavors and responsible with so many commitments that we often end up feeling like we're failing at all of it. Let's encounter Jesus in this devotional as He collides with Mary and Martha in **Luke 10**.

In this 7-part study we will see the invitation Jesus extends to these two women who were both tempted by distractions, worry, comparison, hustle, striving, and more. We are certain that as you walk through this guided reflection written by a team of amazing women, you will deeply connect with Jesus, gain wonderful insight, experience peace and restoration, and understand more of what Jesus means when He says "she has chosen what is best." Friend, our hope is that as you face the myriad of choices each and every day that you would be able to filter through all the voices, all the demands, all the temptations, all the pressures and choose what's best. **Lets' collide…**

2

The Lord and his disciples were traveling along and came to a village. When they got there, a woman named Martha welcomed him into her home. She had a sister named Mary, who sat down in front of the Lord and was listening to what he said. Martha was worried about all that had to be done. Finally, she went to Jesus and said, "Lord, doesn't it bother you that my sister has left me to do all the work by myself? Tell her to come and help me!"

The Lord answered, "Martha, Martha! You are worried and upset about so many things, but only one thing is necessary. Mary has *chosen what is best*, and it will not be taken away from her."

Luke 10:38-42 CEV

3

Perfectionism

SECTION ONE

by Jillian DeBritz

But he said to me, "My grace is sufficient
for you, for my power is made perfect
in weakness." Therefore I will boast all
the more gladly about my weaknesses, so
that Christ's power may rest on me.

2 Corinthians 12:9

Jillian DeBritz *is a wife, a mom, a writer, personal development coach, and a recovering perfectionist who longs to offer hope and build courage through the words she writes. She is fighting to disarm shame through vulnerably sharing her own journey toward emotional, physical, mental, and spiritual wholeness. Her current faves include reading a new book, singing off-key Broadway hits, chocolate in any form, running outside, caramel americanos with cream, dance parties in the kitchen, and snuggling with her favorite people.*

THE PERFECT HOSTESS: *Martha's Story*

My eyes dart around the kitchen and I see potatoes to be peeled, greens to be washed, wine to be poured, and candles to be lit. *There is still so much left to do.* My chest tightens and I take a deep breath to fight the sense of overwhelm, focusing instead on what to tackle first.

Everything has to be just right.

The sound of laughter draws my attention toward the other room, where a crowd of visitors gathers around our most honored guest—the Teacher, Jesus. Men sit all around Him, some reclining in chairs and some on the floor, but all are listening intently. *What is He saying to them?* I strain my ears to pick up the sound of His voice, moving a little closer and trying to read His smiling lips.

Then I see her. Mary, my sister, sits on the floor at His feet, gazing up at Him and soaking up His every word. A prick of jealousy shoots through my chest at the sight of her. *Doesn't she know her place?* Women are expected to serve unseen, not to receive instruction from a rabbi—let alone sit at His feet in the posture of a disciple. *Who does she think she is?* But Jesus doesn't seem to mind. He looks at her with tenderness in His eyes, and I push down my longing to go sit next to her. I turn back to the potatoes and start peeling, shaving off the thick skin with rough strokes, exposing the white flesh inside. Perfect, I tell myself. *Everything's got to be perfect. Maybe then the Teacher will look at me like that too.*

Reflect

How much do you struggle with the idea that everything has to be "perfect"?

How does believing everything has to be just right affect your life?

A PROTECTIVE BARRIER: *My Story*

It started out innocently enough, the high expectations I learned to hold for myself. I simply wanted to be the best I could be, making the most of every opportunity. *What's wrong with that?* But working hard to get good grades wasn't enough, I decided that I needed straight A's. Making the team wouldn't do, I had to be a starter and a captain. As I received attention and praise for my achievements, every success reinforced the cycle: *Work hard, perform well, and you'll be seen.* Not just seen, but admired. Accepted. Loved. What began as a desire to give my best morphed quickly into an unquenchable drive to be perfect.

It seeped into every area of my life: If I didn't excel in my field, how could I hope for new opportunities at work? If I missed a birthday, who would want to be my friend? If I gained five more pounds, how could I show my face in public? If I didn't pray enough, read my Bible enough, or trust God enough, how could I expect Him to show up for me?

My preoccupation with meeting my own impossible standards slowly created an invisible barrier between myself and others, and even with God. I didn't want to ask for help, to reveal weakness, or to admit how much I didn't know, because I'd convinced myself that my value came from my ability to do all things well. I thought if I could be perfect, no one could find any reason to criticize me. And then no one, including Jesus, could find any reason to reject me.

Perfectionism became my shield from the shame I felt inside, protecting me from the deeply rooted fear that I was inherently unworthy of love or belonging. But focusing on my performance—in my relationships, in my appearance, and even in my ministry—kept me from seeing the One who wanted me just as I was. By spending my energy trying to earn the approval of others, I was missing the affection of God right in front of me. I longed to be seen, accepted, and loved, but didn't realize that I already was.

Reflect

How do you try and find worth in your performance?

How often do you find yourself seeking the approval of others rather than the affection of God?

ATTENTION OVER PERFECTION: *Mary's Story*

Like Martha when she poured herself into her preparations, I often became consumed by things that distracted me from the presence of God in my midst.

Always quick to take action, Martha seemed more comfortable doing things for Jesus than sitting still with Him (**John 11:20, 12:2**). To be sure, Martha's hospitality was a precious offering as she poured her energy into creating a beautiful meal for her beloved friend and His followers. But Jesus sees beyond our performance and into our hearts (**1 Samuel 16:7**).

What thoughts were consuming Martha's attention? What shame nipped at her heels, driving her to compulsively prepare, distracting her from the approval that was already hers? What was she believing about herself and where her value came from?

Jesus spoke gently to her, calling her by name. *"My dear Martha, you are worried and upset over all these details! There is only one thing worth being concerned about"* (**Luke 10:41-42 NLT**). He reminded her of what was essential: not a perfect meal, a perfect home or perfect hospitality, but like Mary, only her full attention.

Similar to Martha, we often feel pressure to prove through our performance that we are enough. So we hustle for our worth, spending time and energy perfecting ourselves in order to quiet the voice of shame, the voice that tells us we're worthless, invisible, unlovable. But no amount of effort will ever be enough. Not gaining the approval of others who are impressed by a perfect meal, flawless body, impeccable décor, or fancy car. Not accruing followers or likes or keeping everyone happy. Not covering grays or removing hair or de-wrinkling skin. Not sticking to the budget or organizing our home. Not even devoting ourselves to ministry or reading the Bible more. Nothing we do will ever make us feel like enough, until we sit in the presence of Jesus and let Him love us just as we are.

Read

● *Psalm 46:10*
● *Psalm 139:1-6*
● *John 15:4-9*

Close your eyes and take a few deep breaths. In your mind's eye, imagine Jesus sitting right in front of you, beaming at you with a smile on His face and a twinkle in His eye. Soak up His delight in you.

Resist the temptation to say anything or do anything for Him. Simply let Him love you for a few moments. Allow yourself to pay attention to His affection for you, just as you are.

If you'd like, you can ask Him if there's anything He'd like you to know. Trust His kind words.

Pray

Take a moment to respond to the moment you just had with God and then ask Him to help give you the strength to lay down Perfectionism and move towards a greater connection with Him.

Journal

Use the following space to journal your thoughts, process feelings brought on by this section, or next steps you're feeling led to take.

_____

_____

_____

_____

_____

_____

_____

_____

_____

_____

_____

_____

_____

People Pleasing

SECTION TWO

by Cynthia Cavanaugh

Whatever you do, work heartily,
as for the Lord and not for men.

Colossians 3:23

Cynthia Cavanaugh *is an author, speaker, and leadership influencer. Her story of brokenness has propelled her to write, teach, and help others redeem their pain and heal through the pages of God's Word. She is an award-winning author of several books, a freelance editor for new authors and is the host of the podcast, The Soul Anchor. Cynthia and her husband live in the Pacific Northwest where they enjoy bicycling and spending time with their grandkids.*

I could hardly believe what I was hearing. "People pleasing? Not me!" I emphatically stated as I sat across from my son and his new bride in a local restaurant. I had been in a 12-step recovery program, and one of our assignments was to give several people a list of our behaviors and ask them which of them best reflected my actions. I didn't see their answer coming, and in response, they both looked at each other and laughed. "Mom, you are a major people-pleaser! You are always wanting to make sure everyone is happy."

Over the next several weeks, God gently prodded me to consider delving into their observations a bit deeper. The story of Mary and Martha in **Luke 10:38-42** decidedly put the stake in the ground. As I read the passage and reflected, I could see myself as Martha in the story. At least until I couldn't.

> *"Now, as they went on their way, Jesus entered a village. And a woman named Martha welcomed him into her house. And she had a sister called Mary, who sat at the Lord's feet and listened to his teaching. But Martha was distracted with much serving. And she went up to him and said, "Lord, do you not care that my sister has left me to serve alone? Tell her then to help me." But the Lord answered her, "Martha, Martha, you are anxious and troubled about many things, but one thing is necessary. Mary has chosen the good portion, which will not be taken away from her."* **Luke 10:38-42**

Let me elaborate. As you read in the collision above, Martha often gets a bad rap. When we hear this passage taught, it's often used in the context of being too busy and forgetting about God. Martha is often portrayed as the villain, and it's insinuated that we should be more like Mary. If you relate more to Martha, it can feel like she is being shamed for serving. And to be fair, it's often because of the way we are directed to interpret Jesus' emphasis in **verse 42**, *"Mary has chosen the good portion, which will not be taken away from her."* Of course, it is always best to choose Jesus, however, I'd like to give us another perspective to consider when it comes to looking at this story through the typical lens of people pleasing.

Being a people pleaser isn't necessarily a bad quality, even though it has a negative connotation in our culture. On the flip side, a people pleaser is recognized for their helpful and caring ways. People pleasing becomes harmful when it is overt and at the expense of others and, as a result, creates a deficit in the helper's life. I think this is what Jesus is trying to express.

First of all, let's give Martha some credit. Hospitality was a significant practice in the Jewish culture and is mentioned often in the New Testament as the criteria for being a faithful follower. Jesus was well known throughout the region and was a prominent figure, and it would be appropriate for Martha to want to prepare a lavish gathering for Him. Besides that, Jesus usually traveled with not only His disciples but several other followers. And remember, there wouldn't necessarily be any way for Martha to know His exact arrival other than a message boy running down the street to the house, yelling, "Jesus is coming!" He was a pop-in guest. It's only fair that Martha might be just a tad out of sorts. There was no Papa Murphy's, Door Dash, or Instacart in the village of Bethany, so a meal would have been prepared from pretty much what you had in your storehouse or could scrape up from your neighbors.

Let's stop a minute and point out what Martha did right. The Bible says she *"welcomed Jesus into her home."* (**verse 38**) She was in task mode because she was intent on showing hospitality to Jesus, an important guest, and His traveling companions. Martha was following the custom of the day to have an open home. Jesus gently speaks to her by saying her name endearingly by repeating it twice. He wasn't rebuking her for being hospitable and wanting to serve Him, but rather He wanted her not to let the worries of the preparations overrule her heart and miss spending time with Him. Presence is more important than performance; that is the underlying message in Jesus calling her out on her complaint about her sister. He was addressing her people-pleasing attitude, which, as Jesus pointed out, involved worry and distraction.

It is when our people pleasing crosses over into performance rather than presence, we become like Martha and miss out on the best that Jesus is offering us in relationship with Him. It isn't our job to make everyone happy in every situation. If you've ever tried to do that, you know how impossible it is and only brings frustration until we cry out like Martha. Rather, **be intent on choosing what is better - practice presence over performance.**

Reflect

Think of a situation or relationship that you tend to go into "people pleasing mode". What motivates you to want to please in those moments?

In what ways do you feel like it's your role to make everyone happy?

What roles or tasks do you find yourself taking on that are not your responsibility?

In the spaces below, think about the last week and the things you did to please others that overwhelmed you.

THINGS I DID TO PLEASE OTHERS:	WHAT WAS MY MOTIVATION TO PLEASE:	HOW IT OVERWHELMED ME:
Ex: Stayed up way too late to make a meal for a friend.	*Ex: I wanted to gain her approval because she didn't invite me to her last party.*	*Ex: I was exhausted the next day and short-tempered with my kids.*

How can you improve your practice of presence over performance?

Make an intentional effort to choose "what is better" by simplifying your steps. What shortcuts can you use to simplify your hospitality plan so that you can be more present with guests?

Pray

Take a moment to pray for God to give you the strength to lay down People Pleasing and move towards a greater connection with Him.

Journal

Use the following space to journal your thoughts, process feelings brought on by this section, or next steps you're feeling led to take.

_____

_____

_____

_____

_____

_____

_____

_____

_____

_____

_____

_____

_____

39

Worry

SECTION THREE

by Joanna Weaver

"*Therefore I tell you, do not be anxious about your life, what you will eat or what you will drink, nor about your body, what you will put on. Is not life more than food, and the body more than clothing? Look at the birds of the air: they neither sow nor reap nor gather into barns, and yet your heavenly Father feeds them. Are you not of more value than they?*"

Matthew 6:25-26

Joanna Weaver *is the bestselling and award-winning author of* Having a Mary Heart in a Martha World, *as well as* Having a Mary Spirit *and* Lazarus Awakening. *A pastor's wife, mother of three, and avid Bible teacher, Joanna loves speaking to women about the powerful freedom that is found in making Jesus Lord and trusting Him for things bigger than themselves. She lives with her family in Hamilton, Montana.*

We bite our fingernails. We pace the floor. We lie awake at night. And all because of worry. Hour after hour, our mental fingers twist around a problem, turning it this way, then that, like a Rubik's Cube. We manipulate and postulate, desperate to solve the puzzle. And yet we seem to find few answers. The sad fact is, we are an anxious people. We are a nation of worriers. "I think there's an epidemic of worry," confirms Dr. Edward Hallowell in his book *Worry*. The best-selling author and psychiatrist estimates that one in four of us-about sixty-five million Americans-will meet the criteria for anxiety disorder at some point in our lifetime. Over half of us are what he calls chronic worriers. But worry is hardly a modern phenomenon. Jesus described precisely the same condition 2,000 years ago. He didn't write a book or establish a clinic. He had no medical degree, but He knew the human heart and soul. Out of the vast knowledge known only to a Creator concerning the created, Jesus spoke truth to a woman caught in chronic worry.[1] *(31-32)*

"Martha, Martha" Jesus observe gently, *"you are worried and upset about many things."* **Luke 10:41**

Why is the Bible so adamant about our avoiding fear and worry? Because God knows worry short-circuits our relationship with Him. It fixes our eyes on our situation rather than our Savior. It works a little like a thick London fog - the kind of fog that is legendary. Why, it wouldn't be a Sherlock Holmes story without fog to obscure the villain and allow him to get away. "Thick as pea soup," Londoners describe it. "Can't see your hand in front of your face," they say. However, while physical fog may seem dense and almost solid, scientists tell us that a fog bank a hundred feet deep and covering seven city blocks is composed of less than one glass of water. Divided into billions of droplets, it hasn't much substance. Yet it has the power to bring an entire city to a standstill. So it is with anxiety. Our mind disperses the problem into billions of fear droplets, obscuring God's face. Taking our anxiety to the Lord is often the last thing we think of when we are spiritually fogged in. And yet only the "Son" has the power to disperse it. Without Him, one fear leads to another, and our lives slow to a painful crawl. *(35)*

[1] Weaver, Joanna. Having a Mary Heart in a Martha World: finding intimacy with God in the busyness of life, 2002. Water Brook Press 2002.

Reflect

How have you seen your mind disperse worry into billions of fear droplets?

What are you currently afraid of?

It's been said that worry is like a rocking chair - it gives you something to do, but it doesn't get you anywhere. One interesting set of statistics indicates that there is nothing we can do about 70% of our worries...

What we worry about:
40% are things that will never happen.
30% are about the past - which can't be changed.
12% are about criticism about others, mostly untrue.
10% are about health, which gets worse with stress.
8% are about real problems that can be solved.[2]

Check which of the following you have found yourself worrying about:

❑ I have worried about a past I can't change.

❑ I have worried about hypothetical criticism.

❑ I have worried about my health in ways that made me more unhealthy.

❑ I have worried about real problems with real solutions.

❑

❑

As you consider your past fret(s), what does the exercise above tell you about what you tend to worry about?

[2] "An Average Person's Anxiety Is Focused on…" quoted in John Underhill and Jack Lewis, comp., Bible Study Foundation Illustration Database, Bible Sutdy Foundation Web site (www.Bible.org).

When it comes down to it, worry is really a waste of time. But it's also more than that. Worry is not only futile, it's actually bad for us. The physical and emotional damage caused by chronic anxiety is well known and well documented. Years ago Dr. Charles H. Mayo of the Mayo Clinic pointed out that worry affects circulation, the glands, the whole nervous system, and profoundly affect the heart. In the years since then, researchers have established connections between chronic worry and weakened immune systems, cardiovascular disease, neurological imbalances, clinical depression, and other physical and psychological dysfunctions, not to mention specific anxiety-related illness such as panic attacks, agoraphobia, and obsessive-compulsive disorders.[3] (34)

Which of the following applies to you?

- ❏ weakened immune system
- ❏ cardiovascular disease
- ❏ neurological imbalances
- ❏ clinical depression
- ❏ panic attacks
- ❏ agoraphobia
- ❏ obsessive-compulsive disorder
- ❏ other _____

All that from worry. No wonder Jesus warned Martha about her anxiety. No wonder the Bible tells us more than 350 times to "fear not."

[3] See Archibald D. Hart, Overcoming Anxiety (Dallas: Word, 1989).

Ruminate

Take a moment to read the following passages and reflect on how often God tells you to not fear.

Do not be afraid... for I am with you. **Genesis 26:4**

Do not be afraid... do not be discouraged, for the Lord your God will be with you wherever you go. **Joshua 1:9**

Do not be afraid... for the battle is not yours, but God's. **2 Chronicles 20:15**

Do not be afraid... the Lord will be with you. **2 Chronicles 20:17**

Do not be afraid... of what you have heard. **Isaiah 37:6**

Do not be afraid... for I myself will help you. **Isaiah 41:14**

Do not be afraid... for I am with you and will rescue you. **Jeremiah 1:8**

Do not be afraid... Since the first day that you set your mind to gain understanding and to humble yourself before God, your words were heard. **Daniel 10:12**

Do not be afraid... There is nothing concealed that will not be disclosed, or hidden that will not be made known. **Matthew 10:26**

Do not be afraid... for your Father has been pleased to give you the kingdom. **Luke 12:32**

Do not be afraid... keep on speaking, do not be silent. **Acts 18:9**

Do not be afraid... I will give you the crown of life. **Revelation 2:10**

What strikes you about the fact that God says "do not be afraid" so often?

The truth is, we were simply not wired for worry. We were not fashioned for fear. And if we want to live healthy lives, we have to find a way to leave our chronic anxiety behind. But beyond our physical well-being, there lies a more pressing spiritual reason not to worry.

When God tells us in the Bible not to worry, it isn't a suggestion. It's a command. Worry and/or anxiety is specifically mentioned twenty-five times in the New Testament alone as something we should avoid.

Don't misunderstand. When Jesus told us not to worry, He wasn't asking us to live in denial, a sugar coated fairy tale. He wasn't telling us there's nothing to be concerned about.

The truth is, we live surrounded by opportunities for fear, anxiety, and worry. Because our world is filled with struggles and real pain, we face legitimate concerns every day. Bad things do happen to good people - and not-so-good people as well. Real problems do occur, usually on a daily basis. People don't act the way they ought to. Relationships falter and sometimes fail. There is potential for pain all around us. And there are certainly things that require concern and action on our part.

Jesus knew this better than anybody. He spent most of His life being harassed and pursued by his enemies. So why did He tell us not to worry? Jesus knew that a life filled with fear has little room left for faith. And without faith, we can neither please God nor draw close to Him for the comfort and guidance we need to face the cares and affairs of everyday life. (*37-38*)

That's something we all need to remember when it comes to this issue of worry. We face legitimate concerns every day of our lives. But instead of fretting, instead of worrying, we need to focus on discerning what we can do (with God's help) and what should be left entirely up to God.

Jesus warned us,
"In this world you will have trouble."
John 16:33

Catch that! He said "you will," not "you might." Troubles come with this earthly territory. *"But take heart!"* Jesus says. *"I have overcome the world."* If we have Jesus Christ as our Lord and Savior, we are not alone. We are *never* alone. When life comes blustering down the street, threatening to huff and puff and blow your house down, we can rest in ease. Because we live within a mighty fortress. Because we are hidden beneath almighty wings. Because we have a stronger older Brother right there beside us. And He's rolling up His sleeves. That's the reason we can leave our worry behind - not because there's nothing to be concerned about, but because we have Someone who can handle them a lot better than we can. (*39*)

Reflect

10 Signs of a Big Worrier (according to Dr. Hollowell)

Check the boxes that apply to you:

❑ You find you spend much more time in useless, non-constructive worry than other people you know.

❑ People around you comment on how much of a worrier you are.

❑ You feel that it is bad luck or tempting fate not to worry.

❑ Worry interferes with your work - you miss opportunities, fail to make decisions, and perform at a lower than optimal level.

❑ Worry interferes with your close relationships-your spouse and or friends sometimes complain that your worry is a drain on their energy and patience.

❑ You know that many of your worries are unrealistic or exaggerated, yet you cannot seem to control them.

❑ Sometimes you feel overwhelmed by worry and even experience physical symptoms such as rapid heart rate, rapid breathing, shortness of breath, sweating, dizziness, or trembling.

❑ You feel a chronic need for reassurance even when everything is fine.

❑ You feel an exaggerated fear of certain situations that other people seem to handle with little difficulty.

❑ Your parents or grandparents were known as great worriers or they suffered from an anxiety disorder.

Exercise

Based on the 10 signs of big worries, mark where you're at on the worry scale below.

1
Chillin'

10
Big Worrier

> *Search me, o God, and know my heart; test me and know my anxious thoughts. See if there is any offensive way in me, and leave me in the way Everlasting.*
>
> **Psalm 139: 23-24**

Top 10 Ways to Tame Your Worry Habit

Circle which of these you needed to hear the most.

10. ***Separate toxic worry from genuine concern.*** Determine if you can do anything about your situation. If so, sketch a plan to handle it (**Proverbs 16:3**).

9. ***Don't worry alone.*** Share your concerns with a friend or a counselor. You may receive helpful advice. Talking your fears out with someone often reveals solutions that were invisible before (**Proverbs 27:9**).

8. ***Take care of your physical body.*** Regular exercise and adequate rest can defuse a lot of worry. When our bodies are healthy, our minds can handle stress better and react more appropriately (**1 Corinthians 6:19-20**).

7. ***Do what is right.*** A guilty conscience can cause more anxiety than a world of problems. Do your best to live above reproach. Take care of mistakes quickly by confessing and seeking forgiveness (**Acts 24:16**).

6. ***Look on the bright side.*** Consciously focus on what is good around you. Don't let yourself speak negatively, even about yourself (**Ephesians 4:29**).

5. ***Control your imagination.*** Be realistic about the problems you face. Try to live in the "here and now" not in the "what might be" (**Isaiah 35: 3-4**).

4. ***Prepare for the unexpected.*** Put aside a cash reserve and take sensible measures so you'll be ready if difficulties arise (**Proverbs 21:20**).

3. ***Trust God.*** Keep reminding yourself to put God in your equation. Then, when fear knocks, you can send faith to answer the door (**Psalm 112:7**).

2. ***Meditate on God's promises.*** Scripture has the power to transform our minds. Look for scriptures that deal with your particular areas of anxiety. Answer life's difficulties with God's Word (**2 Peter 1:4**).

1. And the number one way to tame a worry habit? ***Pray!*** Joseph M. Scriven's hymn says it all: *"O what peace we often forfeit, / O what needless pain we bear, / All because we do not carry / everything to God in prayer"*[4] (**Colossians 4:2**). (*47*)

56 [4] Joseph M Scriven, "What a Friend We Have in Jesus," The Hymnal for Worship & Celebration (Waco, Tex.: Word Music, 1986), 435.

Pray

Take a moment to pray for God to give you the strength to lay down the Worry and move towards a greater connection with Him.

Journal

Use the following space to journal your thoughts, process feelings brought on by this section, or next steps you're feeling led to take.

Comparison

SECTION FOUR

by Willow Weston

A heart at peace gives life to the body, but envy rots the bones.

Proverbs 14:30

Willow Weston *is an author, speaker, podcast host, and the Founder and Director of Collide. She has been in ministry for 25 years and loves bringing passion, truth, authenticity and story into every room she walks into. She authentically shares her story of pain, and the beauty that comes out of it, in a way that inspires and encourages people to bravely invite Jesus into their own brokenness so they can experience hope and healing too. Willow, a mom and wife for over 20 years, is as real as it gets, obsessed with throwing parties, coffee, the beach, sunsets, kid cuddles, and a good, good story.*

One of the things we see building up in Martha is comparison. In all her worry and striving and hustle, Martha clearly wants to feel good about who she is and what she's chosen. She looks over at Mary who is chilling with Jesus while she's doing all the work. So she tattles on her sister thinking that Jesus will prop her and knock Mary. She says, *"Lord, don't you care that my sister has left me to do the work by myself? Tell her to help me!"* (**Luke 10:40**) As we know, Jesus doesn't give her the response she was hoping for. The comparison trap rarely makes us feel good nor does it lift up others.

Spend time reading my top 13 pieces of advice when it comes to the comparison game and be open to what God might be saying to you.

☐ *1* **Trust that you are meant to be and then declare it.** If you are **finding** yourself struggling with comparing yourself to others - **your look**s to theirs, your house to theirs, your love life to theirs, **your spirit**uality to theirs - the number one thing you can start to do is trust that God made you. You have life and breathe and are here for a reason and not only that but God made you uniquely as you are and then declare it.

Trust and declare that God made you wonderful. You were uniquely made to put your own print on the world. Your own spin. It's the way you make people feel in a room. It's the way you think. It's the way you write one-liners. It's the way you thrift. It's the way you can sell sawdust to a lumber mill. It's the way you ask good questions. It's the way you discern character. It's the way you serve people. It's the way you show up uniquely you.

"For you created my **inmost** being; you knit
me together in my mother's womb. I praise you
because I am fearfully and wonderfully made; your
works are wonderful, I know that full well. My
frame was not hidden from you when I was made
in the secret place, when I was woven together in
the depths of the earth. Your eyes saw my unformed
body; all the days ordained for me were written
in your book before one of them came to be."

Psalm 139:14-16

☐ **2** **Be confident in your ingredients.** I like to think we're all made with certain ingredients… Sometimes I imagine God almost as if He has a workroom with shelves, all full of different parts or ingredients. And when I'm looking at someone that I'm blown away by because they have giftings that just aren't me, I find myself saying, "God sure didn't go that same shelf He made them with when He made me." They can do technical things or fast-paced number crunching. They can react to emergency situations with ease. They can let haters and their comments slide right on by. They can nurse people back to health. They can organize files and systems and pantries. God went to a shelf when He made them that He didn't go to when He made me. I have learned to be okay with that. My mantra when I start to compare has become, "I am not her, I am me." I need "hers" in my life and she needs me. The same is true for you. God didn't go to every shelf when He made you. You don't have all the giftings, but you certainly have some! Be confident in the ingredients God included in you when He made you.

☐ **3** **If you spend your whole life trying to be like Suzy, you'll never get to be like you.** The longer you spend trying to be like someone else, the longer you put off being you. Until you fully are you, you won't fully be used to impact the world in the way you're made to. Think about all the years you've wasted feeling insecure and unconfident, and even held back because you thought you needed to be like someone else. You can't get those years back, you can't get those opportunities back. But you can start today being you instead of trying to be her.

☐ **4** **Trust God didn't forget about you.** One Christmas Eve in college I showed up unexpectedly to visit one of my parents and they were all opening gifts and when they got done they looked at me and said, "Oh we're sorry, we don't have any gifts for you because we didn't know you were coming." There is a long history of context here that I won't go into now, but you can imagine how I felt. I felt jealous of the other kids who received gifts. To be fair, this side of my family didn't know I was coming. But it was Christmas and the fact that there was nothing for me made me feel so forgotten.

Sometimes I think we think our Heavenly Father forgot about us... like everyone else has giftings and abilities, everyone else has a great calling, and everyone else has a cool personality, but God must have forgotten about me.

God's not like that... God isn't going to remember everyone else and forget you. God is the perfect Father. He is unable to forget about His children. He knows you, He loves you, He's got His eye on **you**. He's got a plan for you. When He made you He didn't forget to **give** you all you need for an amazing life.

☐ **5 Think about how ludicrous it would be if we were all the same.** **If** God is going to use us collectively to impact the world, we can't **all** be the same. We need accountants and we need teachers, we **need** sponsors for those in recovery and we need doctors. We **need** bakers and comedians. We need judges and lawyers and we need singers and poets. God wants to infiltrate all spaces of the world with His people actively sent using their gifts, their story, their experiences, and their own unique way to bless and love the people they collide with. If we all work for the church, if we all are mathematicians, if we all are Instagram influencers, God's hope and love and good news will not be dispersed into all nations, neighborhoods and workplaces. So rather than thinking what she's doing is super cool and wishing it was what you are supposed to be doing, trust that your difference is what God uses.

☐ **6 Refrain from gift envy.** So often we are envious of someone else's **bod**y, family, marriage, career, or house. We are also envious of **the**ir giftings. We wish we had their voice, their sense of humor, **the**ir woo factor, their charisma, their smarts, their self-assuredness, **and** their leadership skills. I will go so far as to say that when you are envious of someone else's God-given gifts, you're stealing from your own God-given gifts. You are outright being ungrateful for the gifts God has given you. Not only that but you are allowing unhealthy thoughts and mindsets to settle in around someone else's God-given abilities. Rather than envy others' gifts, celebrate them.

☐ *7* **Stop comparing someone else's best with your worst.** This is social media's big lie. You are looking at her thousands of followers and your 37 likes. You are looking at her best pic that she probably tried capturing 100x while you look in the mirror and it's been a few days since you've showered. You're looking at her getaway with her besties while you look at your blank weekend calendar. You're looking at her seemingly perfect marriage while you're looking at your husband's ripped underwear. You're looking at her successful career while thinking about leaving yours. The biggest lie about social media is that people are purposely posting what they want you to see, not always what is real. We don't post a picture of our teenager flipping us off. No, we post the sweet two minutes everyone posed for a pic on the beach. We don't post a snapshot of our job review with a list of things we need to improve. No, we post a project we rocked and fail to leave out the things we failed at. We don't post sharing about our deep-rooted feelings of insecurity about the girl who seems to have it all. No, we try to post something that competes with her's in cool factor. If you are struggling with comparing yourself to other people and feeling like you're coming up short, my best advice is to take a social media vacay. See how you feel after one week off from scrolling other people's lives, comparing their best with your worst. If you feel great, maybe you should take a longer vacay. If nothing else, have boundaries with the images that get you down every day and be very self-aware, connecting your social media surf with your inner feelings.

☐ *8* **Give up envy bashing.** There's this thing we do, and we need to call a spade a spade. We see a post of someone we are envious of. It's like everything she touches turns to gold. And we start to do that thing… "Oh my gosh, I think she has an eating disorder, look at how caved in her cheeks are." Or "OMG, she is so privileged, how dare she celebrate her wins. Everything she has was handed to her on a silver platter." Or "Of course, she's sharing her work trip to Florida. She has to brag because she probably slept her way to the top." We tend to bash people we are envious of. So if I may be straight up, she is God's kid. She was made in the image of God. God loves her. She is God's daughter. And God has a plan for her

> *"Let each one examine his own work.*
> *Then he can take pride in himself and not*
> *compare himself with someone else."*
>
> **Galatians 6:4**

life. So you bashing someone else who's trying to do their best because you don't like your best… that's your insecurity making it's home in your heart and getting way too comfortable.

Assess how often you don't like someone because their presence makes you feel less than. Be honest, if this is you, that's your issue, not theirs. There's a saying and I don't know who said it: "Don't ruin other people's happiness just because you can't find your own." If you have been doing some envy bashing, it's a great indicator that you might not be happy and if you're not happy, that's not her issue, that's yours.

73

☐ **9** **Evaluate your use of comparison statements.** We often evaluate ourselves in comparison to others. Examples of comparison statements sound like:

- I'm not an expert like Julie but...
- I'm "just" a stay-at-home mom...
- I'm not a man, so...
- Man, her thighs make mine look like...
- I'm no blogger, but...
- Girl, you're making me look bad...
- Your husband makes my husband look like a lazy bum...
- You have so many more friends than me...

Start paying attention this week to how often you make statements that compare you to another. Theodore Roosevelt called comparison "the thief of joy." Once you locate you have a comparison problem, and you begin battling it, your joy meter will increase.

☐ **10** **Spend more time thinking about what you do have than what you don't.** We are so busy wanting what she has that we can't see what we have. Our jealousy, insecurity and envy steal our gratitude. (Enrich your gratitude with **A 20 Day Walk Toward Gratitude**). Spend time daily locking into gratitude. If you swap envy for gratitude, your joy, your health, your relationships, your dreams, and your goals will all blossom.

☐ **11** **Stop being threatened by other people's greatness.** "Her" greatness doesn't steal from yours. In fact, her greatness could peek yours. It's not like there's a greatness bucket and God has a limited supply. God wants to dole out greatness but your hands need to be open to receive from Him. If you're too busy cross-armed and pouting because of what someone else got, you're going to miss God's greatness hand out to you.

☐ 12 You can never go wrong if you look to be like Jesus instead of looking to be like others. You can admire and respect people. You can learn from people, You can take notes and gain wisdom from people. But if you're trying to be like people, at the end of the day you won't be like them because you are not them. You can say, "I'll never have her body, I'll never have her money, I'll never have her smarts, I'll never have her privilege. But there is one thing you can have and that's Jesus' likeness.

Philippians 2:5-11 says,

"In your lives you must think and act like Christ Jesus. Christ himself was like God in everything. But he did not think that being equal with God was something to be used for his own benefit. But he gave up his place with God and made himself nothing. He was born to be a man and became like a servant. And when he was living as a man, he humbled himself and was fully obedient to God, even when that caused his death -- death on a cross. So God raised him to the highest place. God made his name greater than every other name so that every knee will bow to the name of Jesus -- everyone in heaven, on earth, and under the earth. And everyone will confess that Jesus Christ is Lord and bring glory to God the Father."

If you're aiming to be like someone, be like Christ.

☐ *13* **Do the work of liking yourself.** Friend, if you are struggling to like yourself, my greatest invitation to you right now is to lean into the work of liking yourself. That is an invitation from God. If that looks like going to counseling to process why you are so darn hard on yourself, pick up the phone and make the appointment. If that looks like you starting to take care of your body because you're torturing it, start doing what you know you need to. If that looks like praying and asking God to help you like who He made, get on your knees, girl and start praying. I don't know what it looks like uniquely for you but I do know that God might be inviting you into healing the thing that makes you not like you. Say "yes" to that invitation.

Reflect

I want to invite you to go back and check the boxes of the wisdom on the previous pages that you most needed to hear.

What do you sense God is saying to you?

What can you do to move from comparison and into a place of contentment, gratitude and trust in your own worthiness?

Pray

Take a moment to pray for God to give you the strength to lay down Comparison and move towards a greater connection with Him.

Journal

Use the following space to journal your thoughts, process feelings brought on by this section, or next steps you're feeling led to take.

_____

_____

_____

_____

_____

_____

_____

_____

_____

_____

_____

_____

_____

Distractions

SECTION FIVE

by Kristen Mattila

"Be still,
and know that I am God."

Psalms 46:10

Kristen Mattila, *former Collide staffer, has been through an incredible season of embracing her imperfections, stretching her faith and watching God use her life in ways that consistently surprised her. A few of Kristen's favorite things are bundles of balloons on birthdays, sparkly shoes, puppies, and organizing fun outings with friends. She is always looking for ways to stay active and move around whether that's running, snowshoeing, playing soccer and tennis, or gathering her tandem bike friends and riding around town. Her prayer is that as women we would live bold and brave lives running hard and fast after what God has called us to do.*

Distractions, they're all around us. We are constantly bombarded by them. The beep of a text message or the ring of a phone call, the endless stream of videos on Tik Tok (for me it's those cute puppy clips or epic soccer move videos that keep me scrolling), the email notifications, and the news updates. Do you find yourself easily distracted? I struggle with it. If you really want to get me distracted, take me on a Target run. I go in with a focused mission of buying toothpaste and laundry detergent and end up distracted with a cart full of items.

There are other types of distractions too, like the emotional ones that shake our focus and move us away from feeling healthy, content, and whole. We often find ourselves distracted by comparison, busyness, insecurity, shame, stress, and more. These are the types of distractions that leave us feeling tired, resentful, overwhelmed, lonely, and disconnected.

Every day our attention gets pulled in a million directions and by the end of the week, we are left pretty caught up and distracted. When I am paying attention to what is distracting me, I start to realize how all the distractions impact my sense of worth, my happiness, my relationships, and my mental health. And, I notice how over-focusing on the distractions keeps me further from healing hurt places than they do actually healing me. I can also see the ways that all of those distractions impact my own mental health, and spiritual relationship with the Lord and can leave me missing out on opportunities for healing.

Reflect

What things distract you? And how does getting distracted impact you?

The story of Mary and Martha paints a very relatable picture of how easy it is to miss the forest for the trees when we get tangled up in distractions. This story begins with two sisters, Mary and Martha.

Let's look at **Luke 10:38-42**,

> *"As Jesus and his disciples were on their way, he came to a village where a woman named Martha opened her home to him. She had a sister called Mary, who sat at the Lord's feet listening to what he said. But Martha was distracted by all the preparations that had to be made. She came to him and asked, "Lord, don't you care that my sister has left me to do the work by myself? Tell her to help me!" "Martha, Martha," the Lord answered, "you are worried and upset about many things, but few things are needed—or indeed only one. Mary has chosen what is better, and it will not be taken away from her."*

Here we see Jesus accepted Martha's invitation. When He arrived in her home, the sisters leaned into two very different types of interactions with Jesus. We see Martha allowing the distractions to turn into frustration and resentment, prompting her question to Jesus. At first, she saw Him and invited Him, but once He got there her focus was on the housework and preparations that needed to be done. Her heart was good and intentions pure, I get it… you have people over and you want to make them feel comfortable and be a good host. But, her focus shifted and that turned her good intentions into bitterness, frustration, and resentment towards her sister.

Jesus re-directed Martha's distracted heart towards what was truly important, *"Martha, Martha,"* the Lord answered, *"you are worried and upset about many things, but few things are needed—or indeed only one. Mary has chosen what is better, and it will not be taken away from her."*

There's plenty to capture our attention and more than enough out there around us to steal our focus. Martha and Mary's story shows us a practical example of what it looks like to have Jesus right in front of you and miss Him because of distractions. I have always found it interesting that, according to a German study by Current Biology, humans do not have the ability to walk in a straight line, from one point to the next, unless they have a focal point in the distance to reference. We will straight up walk in circles, around and around. No matter how hard we try, we can't get from point A to B without a focal point.

Martha wanted to see and know Jesus. She loved Him and invited Him, but in a small moment of taking her eyes off him, her focus was interrupted by distractions. We see in the story how that created tension and frustration. The dictionary defines distraction as, "something we do that moves us away from what we really want," and that's exactly what distractions can do to us in our lives. They push us away from the One who can help us shoulder our burdens, restore our hearts and calm our spirits. We need Jesus to be our focal point if we are going to silence the distractions thrown at us each and every day.

So, how do we begin to wade through the distractions and reset our focus on Jesus? On the next page you'll find some reflective practices that are helpful in pinpointing what's causing the distraction and then there is space to discover tools that will help you replace the distractions with something more life-giving. I like having practices that I can turn to when my wandering heart starts to bend more towards distraction instead of connection with God. My hope for you and for me is that we'll begin to re-focus on Jesus and find peace in the midst of all the distractions.

Reflect

Three steps to quiet distractions and gain a connection with God:

1 Right now, find a quiet space with no distractions. This could be a comfy chair, a park bench, or a kid-free car. Wherever you are, put your phone away, turn off the TV or radio and get cozy. Use this time to be intentional about slowing down your pace of life, disengaging from distractions and to-do lists, and reconnecting with God.

2 Take a few minutes to invite the Holy Spirit to center your heart, calm your mind, and quiet the distractions. Close your eyes. Take a few deep breaths and just BE STILL. Use this time to ask the Lord to reveal any patterns in your life that may be distracting you from time with Him.

3 Fill out the chart on the next page by pinpointing areas in your life that may be causing distraction and keeping you from spending time with Jesus and others. When you can be more aware and notice when it's happening, you'll be better able to change course and re-direct your time and attention.

WHAT IS CURRENTLY DISTRACTING ME?

Scrolling on social media…

WHAT DO I REALLY WANT?

A life that feels meaningful and purposed…

HOW DO MY DISTRACTIONS GET IN THE WAY OF WHAT I REALLY WANT?

They cause me to waste time focusing on things that are meaningless and steal my time being purposed…

WHAT I CAN DO TO INTENTIONALLY FOCUS ON JESUS/OTHERS?

Journaling out my thoughts…

Pray

Take a moment to pray for God to give you the strength to lay down Distractions and move towards a greater connection with Him.

Journal

Use the following space to journal your thoughts, process feelings brought on by this section, or next steps you're feeling led to take.

Needed

SECTION SIX

by Michelle Holladay

The God who made the world and everything in it is the Lord of heaven and earth and does not live in temples built by human hands. And he is not served by human hands, as if he needed anything. Rather, he himself gives everyone life and breath and everything else. From one man he made all the nations, that they should inhabit the whole earth; and he marked out their appointed times in history and the boundaries of their lands. God did this so that they would seek him and perhaps reach out for him and find him, though he is not far from any one of us.

Acts 17:24-27

Michelle Holladay *believes passionately in God's word and loves helping others discover how relevant the Bible is to our everyday lives. Her ideal day would be spent on a warm beach with a good book. One day, she blinked and her two children were grown, but being a mom will always be her favorite job, one she has happily shared with her husband of 30 years. Michelle is a former Collide staffer and has led many Collide Bible studies and contributes regularly to the Collide blog as well as other writing projects.*

"Martha, Martha," the Lord answered, *"you are worried and upset about many things, but few things are needed—or indeed only one. Mary has chosen what is better, and it will not be taken away from her."*
Luke 10:41-42

We all know the story. We all know Mary chose better. She should be applauded for her choice and held up as the amazing example she is. But, when I read this story, the person I more easily relate to is Martha. I can see the scene so clearly in my mind. Martha hears that Jesus is planning to come to her house and she is filled with excitement. She wants so desperately to show her Savior that He is loved and valued and worshiped in her home. She thinks of all the things she can do to show Him how much she adores Him, and how grateful she is for Him. I see her begin to make plans and preparations to make sure His visit is perfect. But somewhere along the way, Martha lost sight of what she said yes to.

This is a pattern I see all too often in my life. I say yes to an opportunity because I am passionate about it and I truly believe it is a place God has called me to serve. My deep desire is to serve Him well, but I so easily lose my focus and get distracted by all the details. I become "worried and upset about many things." I find myself losing sleep because I can't shut my brain off from all the tasks that need to be done. I'm frustrated by the people who aren't helping and I feel resentful because nobody notices all the hard work I'm doing. It doesn't take long for me to forget why I said yes in the first place. Simply put, I begin to focus more on what I am doing instead of Who I am serving.

In one of his sermons from the 1870's, Charles Spurgeon said it this way: *"The fact is, the Martha spirit spoils all because it gets us away from the inner soul of service; … we cease to do work as to the Lord, we labor too much for the service sake; the main thing in our minds is the service and not the Master; we are cumbered, and He is forgotten."* [5]

108[51, 2] Spurgeon, C. H. (1870). Martha and Mary. In The Metropolitan Tabernacle Pulpit Sermons (Vol. 16, pp. 235–236). London: Passmore & Alabaster.

It's not a huge surprise we do this. It's natural for us to put stock in what we can see and feel and hear, and this is precisely why we need to take a good, hard look at what is different about Mary's response. I'm sure Mary had the same excitement as Martha and I bet she also wanted to show Jesus how much He was loved and valued and adored. But when Jesus arrived, instead of being worried and upset about the many things she could do for Jesus, Mary remembered the reason she and Martha had said yes to His visit in the first place, to be in the presence of Jesus. Charles Spurgeon elaborates: *"Mary is much wiser when she feels, 'He desires me to receive his words, and yield him my love; I would gladly give him meat, but he will see to that; he is the Master of all things, and can do without me or Martha. I need him far more than he can need me.'"* [5]

This idea that I need God far more than He needs me was revealed more clearly to me one day while I was praying in my car. Once again, I found myself in the midst of ministry, "worried and upset about many things." All of a sudden, it was like this sermon by Charles Spurgeon popped into my head that said, "God does not need you for this. He doesn't need you for anything. He is GOD, the same God who created the heavens and the Earth with a word, the same God who makes the blind see and the lame walk, the same God who fed 5,000 hungry people with 5 loaves of bread and 2 fish. He did all this through His own power. Sure, He let humans participate in some of these miracles, but He did not need them. When Moses put his staff into the Red Sea to part the waters, it was not the staff in the water that made the miracle happen, it was all God."

Well, this little mini-sermon stopped me in my tracks. If God did not need Moses, if God does not need me, then what must be true is HE WANTS ME. This was life-changing. I had forgotten that when I said yes, I said yes to the presence of Jesus. I said yes to helping create a space for women to sit at His feet and that included me. I had forgotten that God is the Master of all things, and is quite capable of doing far more than I could ever imagine without my help. But what an awesome privilege it is that He wants me to be a part of His work.

Reflect

How do you see yourself living like God needs you versus God wants you?

When I began to look at the work God calls me to through this lens, my whole perspective changed. My ego wants to believe I am necessary, that I provide a service nobody else can provide. But how much more gratifying is it to know that despite not being needed, I am actually wanted? How could I have any other response but to choose the better yes and fall at Jesus' feet?

I used to cringe at the rebuke Jesus gives Martha, but recently I read that "some commentators take the repeated *'Martha, Martha'* of **verse 41** as an indication that Jesus' seeming rebuke is, in fact, a call to discipleship". Perhaps the best evidence for this is when God calls to Moses from the burning bush or when Jesus says to Paul, *"Saul, Saul, why do you persecute me?"* (**Acts 9:4**). I find this to be a beautiful thought, this idea of Jesus gently repeating Martha's name, calling her into deeper fellowship with Him. It's as if He wants her to know that He truly sees her and He knows her heart and He knows what she is capable of and all she has to do is choose a better yes.

What might change for us if we began to see Jesus' discipline as less about Him calling us out and more about Him calling us in to something deeper? What if you heard Him gently repeating your name and saying, "you are worried and upset about many things but remember why you said yes to my invitation in the first place. **I see you. I choose you. I want you.** Won't you come and sit at my feet? Won't you trust that I can do infinitely more than you could ever ask or imagine? Won't you choose a better yes?"

Reflect

Place yourself in the room with Mary and Martha…what is Mary receiving in this moment? And what is Martha receiving?

MARY	MARTHA

If Jesus wants both Mary and Martha to know they're loved and chosen, what do they each have to do to receive it?

Pray

Take a moment to pray for God to give you the strength to lay down your need to be Needed and move towards a greater connection with Him.

Journal

Use the following space to journal your thoughts, process feelings brought on by this section, or next steps you're feeling led to take.

The Hustle

by Krista Brielh

"Come to me, all you who are weary and burdened, and I will give you rest. Take my yoke upon you and learn from me, for I am gentle and humble in heart, and you will find rest for your souls."

Matthew 11:28-29

Krista Breilh *is the Founder and Executive Director of a ministry called Live Salted. Krista is a lover of the hypothetical and playing with the what if's, she loves to dream big, and her goal is to live a life so reliant upon the Lord, where if He doesn't show up it's embarrassing. You'll find her often speaking and writing about how Jesus has come to give us life, and life to the fullest. She loves adventuring outside, drinking kombucha, and connecting with strangers whenever she goes.*

Hustle can be rationalized, but should it? We live in a culture of hustle. The evidence is all around us, and frankly, it's undeniable. One of the hardest parts about the hustle is that we are quick to rationalize our efforts:

- *They would feel so loved if I **just**...*
- *I would be such a better leader/spouse/friend/parent if I **just**...*
- *It would feel so good if I **just**...*
- *I think I have **just** enough time to...*
- *If I **just** get one more thing done then I will be...*

Let's look again at the circumstances of Martha and see how hustle plays into how she carried herself that day Jesus came over. If Jesus were coming over to your house to dine, wouldn't you want your house to be cleaner than ever? Wouldn't you display the most eloquent and thoughtful assortment of food and beverages for when He arrived? And wouldn't you want to share the responsibility of getting ready for this holy house guest to be shared with those around you?

I know I would! And I am guessing most of you would as well.

What is the root emotion of your hustle? As we can see Martha was feeling some emotions. In **Luke 10:40** she says, *"Lord, don't you care that my sister has left me to do the work by myself? Tell her to help me!"* Hustle can and will feel different to us all, and more importantly, it will vary from season to season. Some of the most common ways I have seen myself and others experience hustle are through the sensations of:

- **Exhaustion** - This is what you feel when the weight of responsibilties fall on your shoulders.
- **Falling Behind** - This is what you feel when you confuse what is needed with what is truly most important.
- **Never Feeling Good Enough** - This is what you feel when you continue to say "yes," putting too much on your plate and never feeling like you're measuring up.
- **Confusion** - This is what you feel when you have spent so much time doing and not enough feeling, thinking, and processing.

Naming our emotions that come up while we hustle is one of the best ways to start walking towards freedom and healing. In the myriad of emotions that hustle brings, I think there is one specific emotion at the root of it all and it is found in the Scripture above. Did you notice what it was? Martha absolutely nailed our biggest worry. We see Martha's root emotion was isolation and loneliness.

Reflect

What are some of the emotions you feel when you hustle?

You feeling isolated and alone was never meant to be the case. The Lord tells us all throughout Scripture that He will never leave us or forsake us (**Hebrews 13:5**), yet why is it so often that we take on that narrative? Why is it so often we feel like we hold the weight of the world when He tells us His yoke is easy and His burden is light (**Matthew 11:28-30**)?

It's because the enemy that works against God, loves for us to feel alone, and will do whatever he can to make that happen. Taken one step further, that same enemy also loves to fill us with pride. He wants us to think we can do it alone and don't need the Lord or anyone else's help. You might be scratching your head wondering how Martha's desire to serve well and work hard is a pride issue, but it comes down to this belief that you are able to do it all and don't need anyone's help, especially God's. *Ooph… that hits me hard.*

Jesus wants to be WITH you in it all. When that sensation of isolation kicks in and you feel the weight of everything on your shoulders, I invite you to consider if you are working WITH Jesus or FOR Him in the moment. And if you are working FOR Him, but not WITH Him, how you might bring back your attention to the reality that Jesus desires to do EVERYTHING with you?

From the outside, not much changes when looking at the difference between working WITH Jesus versus FOR Jesus, but from the inside, the mindset is entirely different. Hustle in itself isn't wrong; however, doing life on your own without connection and reliance on the Spirit is.

Jesus doesn't just want to be a pit stop during our quiet time or a quick "help me" prayer in the car. He wants to meet us and never leave our side from that moment on. He wants to be with us as we prepare for that big meeting with our bosses and then, never leave our side all day. He wants to dwell with us as we pray over our relationships and friendships. He wants to reside with us when we bring up hard topics or conversations. He wants to sit in all the emotions you listed above and simply say, I'm WITH you.

Reflect

What does it look like for you to work WITH Jesus instead of FOR Him?

When you feel alone in your hustle, what can you do?

When you feel pride that you can do it all, what can you do?

Pray

Take a moment to pray for God to give you the strength to lay down
The Hustle and move towards a greater connection with Him.

Journal

Use the following space to journal your thoughts, process feelings brought on by this section, or next steps you're feeling led to take.

_____

_____

_____

_____

_____

_____

_____

_____

_____

_____

_____

_____

_____

Way to choose what's best!

You did it! You finished walking through the collision between Jesus, Mary and Martha! Our hope is that you experienced a deeper love of Jesus and sensed His nudge to slow down and make space for more of His presence in your life. We know that you will continue to live in a world that begs your attention and invites your distraction, but we hope that you will say bye-bye to comparison and perfectionism, people pleasing and fret. We hope that you will experience more peace, more purpose, more grace, and more of Jesus in your life as you choose what is best.

As you walk away from this experience, we hope that you will keep colliding with Jesus. We are certain that the more you run into Him, the more you are transformed. Around Collide, we make it our aim to create more ways you can do just that. So make sure you check out all our content, podcasts, blogs, Bible study books, online courses, conferences, and more. We want to help you continue to grow and heal in Jesus.

Keep colliding, friend!

xoxo,
The Collide Team

Acknowledgments

This project was a collective work of some amazing women getting together and trusting God could use the sum of what we have to do something big. I am so very grateful for these women who poured out their energy, leaned into their giftings, gave of their time, and made great sacrifices to craft this project and get it into the hands of those we believe it will impact. God calls His people the Body, and as I like to say, God gave Collide one hot body! These beautiful women are the hands and feet, the heart and mind, the lungs and mouthpiece being used to bless the world around them and for that, I am truly grateful. There is nothing greater than together handing God what we have and seeing what He can do!

~ Willow

Guest Contributors
Perfectionism by Jillian DeBritz
People Pleasing by Cynthia Cavanaugh
Worry by Joanna Weaver
Comparison by Willow Weston
Distractions by Kristen Mattila
Needed by Michelle Holladay
The Hustle by Krista Brielh

Staff Acknowledgements
Content Contributor: Kerstin DeNeui
Layout and Proofreading: Kim Taddonio
Editor: Anna Kuttel
Photography: Emily Gish
Graphic Design: Amanda Garvin

come collide.
with us

We have more ways you can collide with Jesus at
wecollide.net

Follow us on social!

@wecollidewomen   @we.collide   @wecollidewomen

Made in the USA
Columbia, SC
04 August 2025

60951604R00082

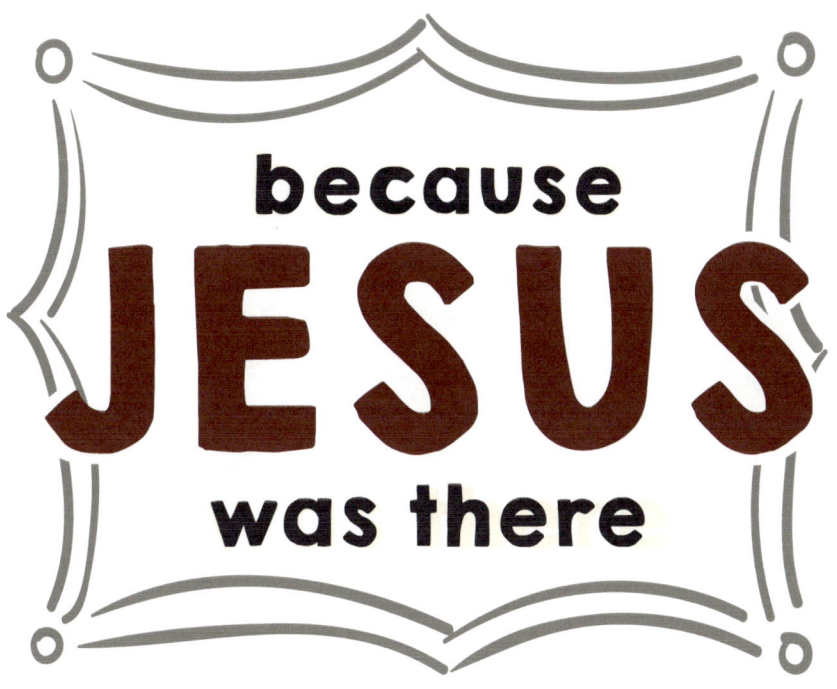

because JESUS was there

by A.M. Everett

illustrated by Ian Mac

ACOMA PRESS

"Children need frequent reminders of Jesus' presence and this beautiful book shares just that. You will feel like you are part of the scene in these captivating illustrations. From his time on earth to his current position in heaven, Jesus is always there with us, and that is a comfort to both the reader and listener!"

TINA TOMAN *Children's Ministry Director (25+ years), Windsor, CO*

"This beautifully illustrated book has sound theology that children can easily understand. The lyrical manner with which it is written is unique and the guiding questions for reflection are extremely helpful. This book is a treasure for all who read it!"

KEVIN & JENN HASENACK *Kevin - Pastor, Calvary Wellspring, Aurora, CO; Jenn - Teacher (18+ years), Aurora, CO*

"One of the biggest blessings of growing up in a Christ-centered home is a long and deep saturation in the gospel. But it is not enough to simply teach children theology as an abstraction. We need to immerse our kids in the wondrous, mind-blowing story of God's work in history, and help them connect the dots to see God working in and around us today. This little book uniquely retells a few key gospel stories and provides a fantastic springboard for dozens of spiritual conversations. More than a storybook, this is a resource for discipleship."

KATE MORGAN *Acoma Press Author and Mother of three*

"This little book has a BIG message: Jesus is always with us! As believers in Christ, we must teach our children that whether life seems too easy or hard, God is 'closer than a brother.' Using powerful biblical stories, *Because Jesus Was There* helps our families reflect on God's omniscience in a way that is accessible to young hearts and minds."

JENNA HALLOCK *Executive Director, Family Time Training*

Copyright © 2022 by A.M. Everett and Ian Mac
Text Copyright © 2022 by A.M. Everett
Illustrations Copyright © 2022 by Ian Mac

Published by
Acoma Press
40 W. Littleton Blvd. Suite 210, PMB 215
Littleton, CO 80120
www.acomapress.org

All rights reserved. No part of this publication may be reduced, stored in a retrieval system, or transmitted in any form by any means, electronic, mechanical, photocopy, recording, or otherwise, without the prior permission of the publisher, except as provided for by USA copyright law.

Interior Layout and Title Design: Evan Skelton

Paperback ISBN: 979-8-9852233-6-1
PDF ISBN: 979-8-9852233-7-8
First Printing, 2022
Printed in the United States of America

DEDICATION

For my precious Henry, Ellis, and Lottie.
You are God's great gift to me.

And for all of the sweet children I'm
blessed to know.

I pray you'll never forget Jesus'
nearness and His love for you.

A big storm was blowing,
we were all in a boat.

We were sure to fall in.
I didn't think I would float.

I was afraid,
more than I've ever been.

But Jesus was there,
and He spoke to the wind.

The waves stopped their crashing.
It was all better now;

Because Jesus was there,
the big storm died down.

When our brother got sick,
we asked Jesus to come;

But it was too late;
death had already won.

How could this happen?
What could we do?

But then Jesus was there,
and He spoke to the tomb.

Our brother walked out
like he'd never been sick!

Because Jesus was there,
our brother lived!

The day they took Jesus
was the scariest yet.

He was nailed to a cross,
a crown of thorns on His head.

Our hero, our friend,
gone forever it seemed...

But then Jesus was there!
A victorious King!

He was stronger than death!
He was stronger than sin!

Because Jesus was there,
our new lives could begin!

I spoke to a crowd.
They yelled and got angry;

They knew I loved Jesus,
so they hated me.

They took off their coats
and picked up some stones.

But then Jesus was there,
    standing up by God's throne!

He was dressed like a King,
    and His bright white clothes shone.

Because Jesus was there,
    I could finally go home!

It's okay to feel scared
when things start to go wrong;

When storms start to blow,
or your friends are all gone.

But Jesus is there.
He's still on His throne;

And His Spirit's right here,
so you're never alone.

His strength is in you,
so just keep walking straight;

Because Jesus is here—
and that won't ever change!

"And behold, I am with you always, to the end of the age."

(Matthew 28:20b)

A NOTE TO PARENTS & CAREGIVERS

These days, many psychologist-recommended books for children are telling our kids, "You are enough. You can be your own hero." As believers in Jesus, we get to teach our kids something different. Something better.

Jesus is our hero, and we have the joy of sharing our hope in Him with our kids. When emotions and circumstances feel too hard to handle, we don't have to be strong. Instead, we can trust in Jesus' strength to carry us through! We pray this book will strike up rich conversations about hardship and the Spirit's presence in our lives.

Use the questions below as a guide for added conversation:

- *When have you been afraid?*
- *Where was Jesus when that was happening?*
- *Do you think He'll ever leave you alone?*
- *What can you do the next time you feel scared?*

ABOUT THE AUTHOR/ILLUSTRATOR

A.M. EVERETT lives in South Asia with her wonderful husband, two sons, and one daughter. Writing is one of her favorite ways to bear God's image in the world, and she hopes to inspire little minds to bear His image to the world in the special and unique talents that God has given them!

IAN MAC has been involved in cross-cultural ministry for 14 years. He is currently blessed to live in South Asia with his beautiful wife and three joyful children. He uses art as a way to Sabbath. Nevertheless, as with all things, it is his desire that God might use it to glorify Himself to the ends of the earth!

See the next page
for a coloring
activity you can
do together!

Have fun coloring these pages together!

Also available from

ACOMA PRESS

"Who is God? What is He like?
I really want to know."

by mark hallock
illustrated by Kyle riggins

Also available from
ACOMA PRESS

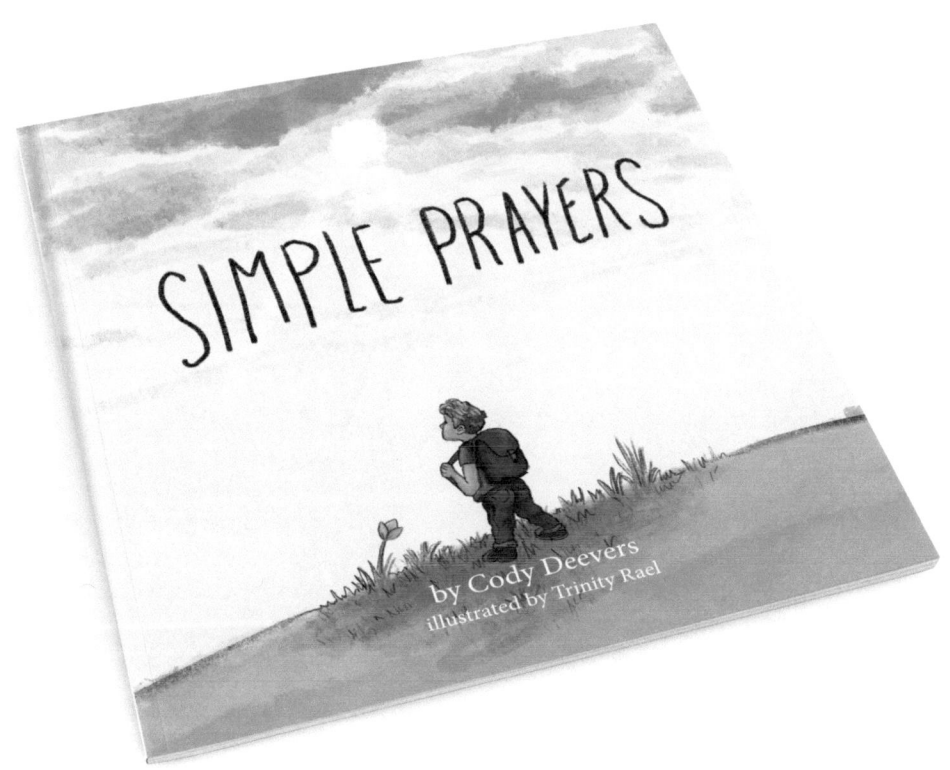

praying to the God who created us,
calls to us, and delights in us

by Cody Deevers
illustrated by Trinity Rael

ACOMA PRESS

Acoma Press exists to make Jesus non-ignorable by equipping and encouraging churches through gospel-centered resources.

Toward this end, each purchase of an Acoma Press resource serves to catalyze disciple-making and to equip leaders in God's Church. In fact, a portion of your purchase goes directly to funding planting and replanting efforts in North America and beyond. To see more of our current resources, visit us at acomapress.org.

Thank you.

Made in the USA
Columbia, SC
04 August 2025

60957013R00015

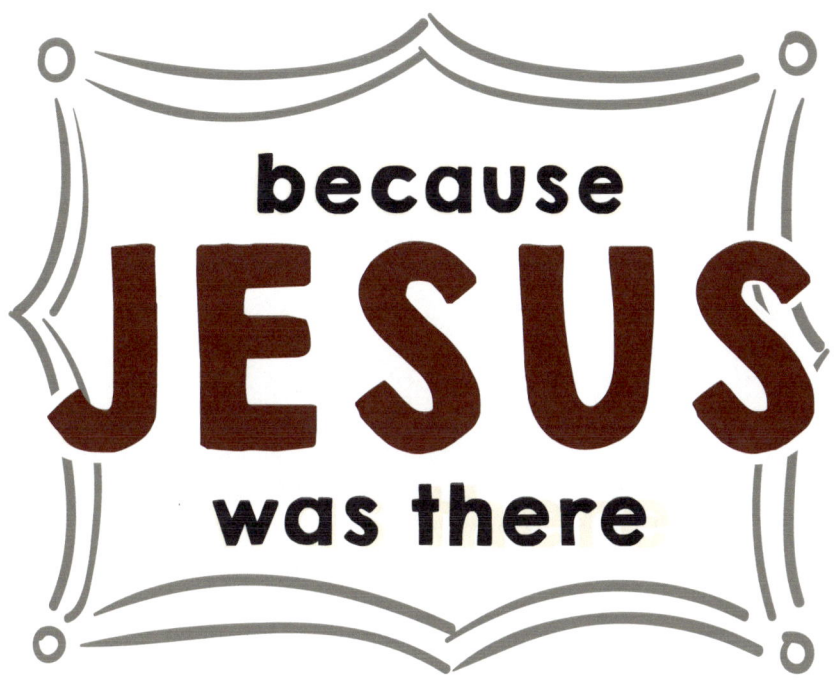

because
JESUS
was there

by A.M. Everett

illustrated by Ian Mac

ACOMA PRESS

"Children need frequent reminders of Jesus' presence and this beautiful book shares just that. You will feel like you are part of the scene in these captivating illustrations. From his time on earth to his current position in heaven, Jesus is always there with us, and that is a comfort to both the reader and listener!"

TINA TOMAN *Children's Ministry Director (25+ years), Windsor, CO*

"This beautifully illustrated book has sound theology that children can easily understand. The lyrical manner with which it is written is unique and the guiding questions for reflection are extremely helpful. This book is a treasure for all who read it!"

KEVIN & JENN HASENACK *Kevin - Pastor, Calvary Wellspring, Aurora, CO; Jenn - Teacher (18+ years), Aurora, CO*

"One of the biggest blessings of growing up in a Christ-centered home is a long and deep saturation in the gospel. But it is not enough to simply teach children theology as an abstraction. We need to immerse our kids in the wondrous, mind-blowing story of God's work in history, and help them connect the dots to see God working in and around us today. This little book uniquely retells a few key gospel stories and provides a fantastic springboard for dozens of spiritual conversations. More than a storybook, this is a resource for discipleship."

KATE MORGAN *Acoma Press Author and Mother of three*

"This little book has a BIG message: Jesus is always with us! As believers in Christ, we must teach our children that whether life seems too easy or hard, God is 'closer than a brother.' Using powerful biblical stories, *Because Jesus Was There* helps our families reflect on God's omniscience in a way that is accessible to young hearts and minds."

JENNA HALLOCK *Executive Director, Family Time Training*

Copyright © 2022 by A.M. Everett and Ian Mac
Text Copyright © 2022 by A.M. Everett
Illustrations Copyright © 2022 by Ian Mac

Published by
Acoma Press
40 W. Littleton Blvd. Suite 210, PMB 215
Littleton, CO 80120
www.acomapress.org

All rights reserved. No part of this publication may be reduced, stored in a retrieval system, or transmitted in any form by any means, electronic, mechanical, photocopy, recording, or otherwise, without the prior permission of the publisher, except as provided for by USA copyright law.

Interior Layout and Title Design: Evan Skelton

Paperback ISBN: 979-8-9852233-6-1
PDF ISBN: 979-8-9852233-7-8
First Printing, 2022

Printed in the United States of America

DEDICATION

For my precious Henry, Ellis, and Lottie.
You are God's great gift to me.

And for all of the sweet children I'm
blessed to know.

I pray you'll never forget Jesus'
nearness and His love for you.

A big storm was blowing,
we were all in a boat.

We were sure to fall in.
I didn't think I would float.

I was afraid,
more than I've ever been.

But Jesus was there,
and He spoke to the wind.

The waves stopped their crashing.
It was all better now;

Because Jesus was there,
the big storm died down.

When our brother got sick,
we asked Jesus to come;

But it was too late;
death had already won.

How could this happen?
What could we do?

But then Jesus was there,
and He spoke to the tomb.

Our brother walked out
like he'd never been sick!

Because Jesus was there,
our brother lived!

The day they took Jesus
was the scariest yet.

He was nailed to a cross,
a crown of thorns on His head.

Our hero, our friend,
gone forever it seemed...

But then Jesus was there!
A victorious King!

He was stronger than death!
He was stronger than sin!

Because Jesus was there,
our new lives could begin!

I spoke to a crowd.
They yelled and got angry;

They knew I loved Jesus,
so they hated me.

They took off their coats
and picked up some stones.

But then Jesus was there,
    standing up by God's throne!

He was dressed like a King,
    and His bright white clothes shone.

Because Jesus was there,
    I could finally go home!

It's okay to feel scared
when things start to go wrong;

When storms start to blow,
or your friends are all gone.

But Jesus is there.
He's still on His throne;

And His Spirit's right here,
so you're never alone.

His strength is in you,
so just keep walking straight;

Because Jesus is here—
and that won't ever change!

A NOTE TO PARENTS & CAREGIVERS

These days, many psychologist-recommended books for children are telling our kids, "You are enough. You can be your own hero." As believers in Jesus, we get to teach our kids something different. Something better.

Jesus is our hero, and we have the joy of sharing our hope in Him with our kids. When emotions and circumstances feel too hard to handle, we don't have to be strong. Instead, we can trust in Jesus' strength to carry us through! We pray this book will strike up rich conversations about hardship and the Spirit's presence in our lives.

Use the questions below as a guide for added conversation:

- *When have you been afraid?*
- *Where was Jesus when that was happening?*
- *Do you think He'll ever leave you alone?*
- *What can you do the next time you feel scared?*

ABOUT THE AUTHOR/ILLUSTRATOR

A.M. EVERETT lives in South Asia with her wonderful husband, two sons, and one daughter. Writing is one of her favorite ways to bear God's image in the world, and she hopes to inspire little minds to bear His image to the world in the special and unique talents that God has given them!

IAN MAC has been involved in cross-cultural ministry for 14 years. He is currently blessed to live in South Asia with his beautiful wife and three joyful children. He uses art as a way to Sabbath. Nevertheless, as with all things, it is his desire that God might use it to glorify Himself to the ends of the earth!

See the next page
for a coloring
activity you can
do together!

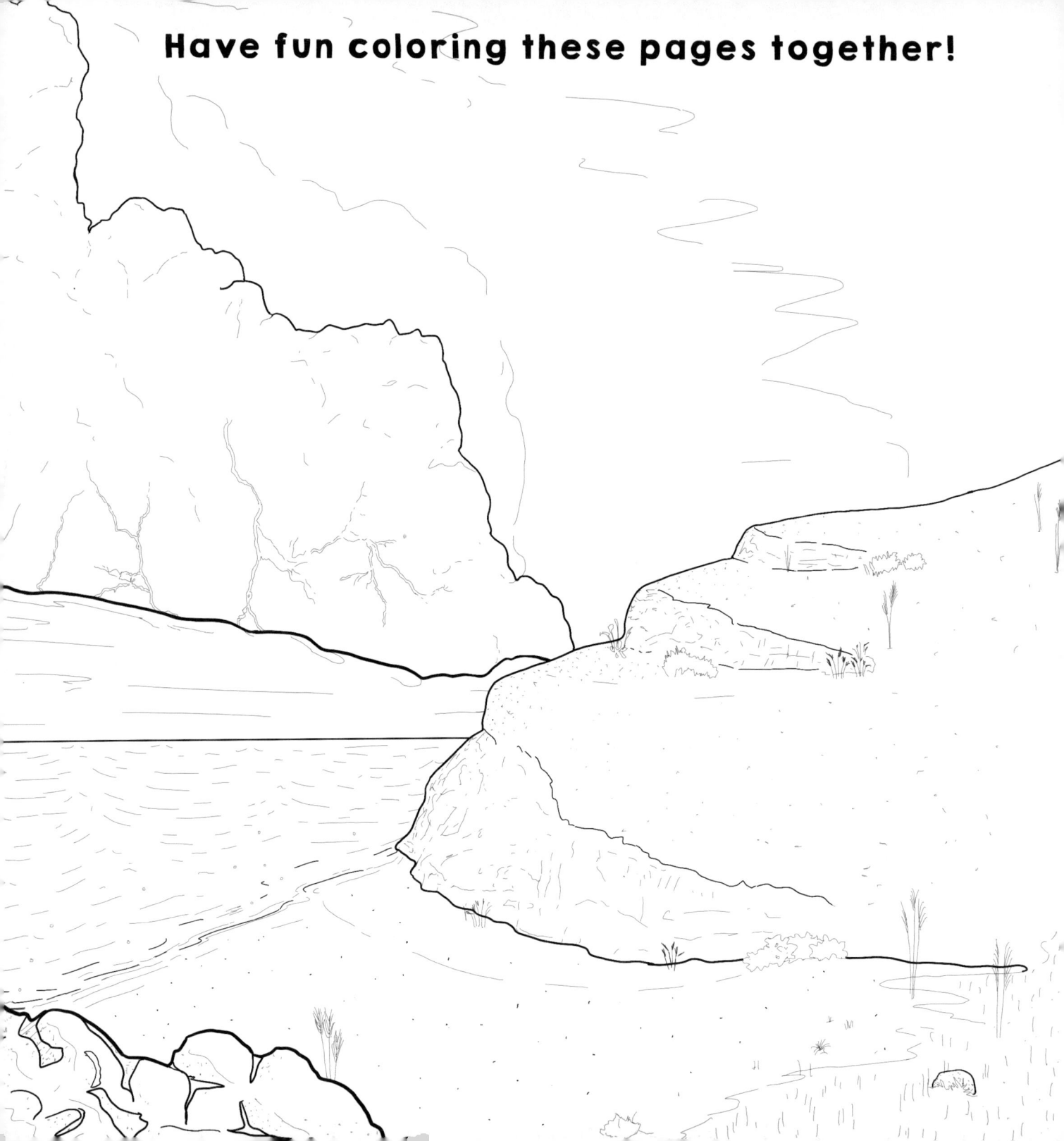

Have fun coloring these pages together!

Also available from
ACOMA PRESS

"Who is God? What is He like?
I really want to know."

by mark hallock
illustrated by Kyle riggins

Also available from
ACOMA PRESS

praying to the God who created us,
calls to us, and delights in us

by Cody Deevers
illustrated by Trinity Rael

ACOMA PRESS

Acoma Press exists to make Jesus non-ignorable by equipping and encouraging churches through gospel-centered resources.

Toward this end, each purchase of an Acoma Press resource serves to catalyze disciple-making and to equip leaders in God's Church. In fact, a portion of your purchase goes directly to funding planting and replanting efforts in North America and beyond. To see more of our current resources, visit us at acomapress.org.

Thank you.

Made in the USA
Columbia, SC
04 August 2025

60957002R00015